READING

Amr Muneer Dahab

authorHOUSE®

AuthorHouse™
1663 Liberty Drive
Bloomington, IN 47403
www.authorhouse.com
Phone: 833-262-8899

Published by AuthorHouse 08/25/2021

ISBN: 978-1-6655-3648-6 (sc)
ISBN: 978-1-6655-3649-3 (e)

To those who adore reading.
To those who are eager to improve and
develop their reading skills.
To those who believe that there are other means
of knowledge more important than reading.

CONTENTS

PREFACE

Reading should not be just a mission. Reading is pleasure.

All that you read solely to help you complete work or as a duty may enable you to achieve that purpose, but there is more to the joy of reading, without which you will miss what should remain forever in your subconscious: inspiration and its manifestations in various aspects of your life.

This book aims to make your relationship with books, and reading in general, one that goes beyond the mere desire to hurry to finish a heavy task, or even the aspiration toward cognitive benefit, to the pure love of reading. When you reconcile with reading and love it, all its desired benefits will flow to you on their own.

THE PURPOSE OF READING

1

One of the loftiest goals of reading is pleasure. If you feel pleasure while reading, you don't need to be in a hurry to find another purpose to justify adoring books.

What is meant by the purposes of reading is ultimately its benefits. And the benefits of reading are limitless.

Knowledge is not the ultimate purpose of reading but a means to many other purposes. Don't worry if these purposes are sometimes not perfectly clear to you as long as you love reading and practice it sincerely.

Reading for the sake of ostentation is, of course, denounced. But sharing ideas and brainstorming are not without benefits. Just choose with whom you share your readings, choose carefully what you share, and listen closely to what others have to say.

📖 The purpose of book discussions is not to arrive at a unified view of what is being presented. Rather, it is to experience an enriched discussion with divergent opinions.

📖 As you seek to know others and their cultures as one of the main purposes of reading, you will be surprised by the no less wonderful gift of getting to know yourself better.

📖 Passing the time is one of the most popular motives for reading among the general public. Don't be shy about admitting it if that sometimes applies to you. Reading to pass the time isn't a disadvantage in and of itself, but the best thing is that you'll be surprised at the many benefits showered on you as you pass your time that way.

📖 Even the academic books that you read for the purpose of passing a particular exam have many benefits that you won't see while thinking about the exam questions. Give the book the opportunity to inspire you later in one way or another when your immediate academic need for it elapses.

📖 The priorities of your reading goals change with age. Each stage of life has its own temperament, and there is nothing to worry about in any way.

📖 To devoted lovers of reading, the purposes of reading seem ultimately to be leading to one another.

WHAT TO READ

2

📖 First of all, everything is readable. Don't begin by placing limits on reading areas. Read in each field, and you will find the most favorable for your reading unfold on its own.

📖 Don't be alarmed if you find yourself reading outside mainstream books and topics. On the contrary, it is wonderful to be taken over by what you love to the point that you dispense with what matters to other people in general.

📖 No reading genre is the best ever. You determine that, according to what you find yourself in need of and attracted to.

📖 The main challenges of diversifying reading topics often lie in the transition from one genre to another. It is a challenge that has its difficulties at times, but it is not without pleasure if you are convinced and genuinely willing to explore the worlds of a genre new to you.

📖 It's important to respond smoothly to age transitions and life's ups and downs, as the mood for reading changes. You may find yourself sometimes becoming more distant from your favorite books and drawn to different readings arenas. These transitions will give you intellectual and spiritual richness and rejuvenate your life, if you pay attention to such transitions intelligently and use them with open horizons.

📖 There is no need to worry when you find yourself reading in only one field for a long time, as long as you enjoy and benefit from it. But it is OK to take the initiative on your own with some changes in the field of reading to see whether you like the new experience.

📖 Don't be in a rush to judge new reading just because you didn't like it at first. Give yourself the chance for a careful and a thoughtful judgment with more patience before you decide to part with that kind of reading for good.

📖 If you did not like a book in a literary genre that is new for you after just one experience, you should still give yourself the opportunity to try again with another book later on. One individual, or even a group of individuals, is not sufficient to make a sound and accurate judgment on the society to which they belong.

📖 When you are fascinated by a new field of reading, there is no need for you to cut off your connection to the field you used to love. What is the problem in combining two beloved genres in the world of reading?

📖 As you are looking to expand your reading circle or go beyond it, do not limit your research only to different genres, but look also at other authors and writings from other countries and different cultures—and feel free to try the most different and strange readings in any field from any country and for any author.

HOW TO READ

📖 Avoid the glut of reading and give your mind the ability to think and analyze.

📖 Reading is a pleasure, and no one has the right to impose on you how to enjoy it. It's OK to get inspiration from others' differing experiences, and you don't have to worry about how to read the "best" way as long as you enjoy what you're reading and look forward to reading more of it.

📖 Don't get too caught up in thinking about how to read a book even if you're a beginner. As soon as you open up a book and start browsing, it will reveal the best way to read it.

📖 Each book offers its own approaches to reading, getting pleasure, and extracting benefits based on many factors. Volume is one of the most significant among these factors.

📖 There is no one way to read all books all the time. Each book inspires how to read it according to the time and place, and most important according to your need and mood as a reader.

The best way to improve your reading is to make use of your own experiences. Always study your previous reading experiences carefully and be both nimble about learning lessons and flexible enough to apply them.

The best way to read a book is the way through which you enjoy reading it. You are the only one who knows for sure whether you are enjoying something or not.

The book you want to read is yours. Every page is yours, every line is yours, every word is yours. Choose how you act with what you own.

Unless you happen to deeply enjoy reading a book until you're done with it, feel free to read more than one book at a time as this should not confuse you. Remember that you used to do this all the time at school.

No matter how old you are and the experience you've gained, don't hesitate to change your way of reading whenever you feel the urge to do so. There will often be a rationale that you don't identify clearly. In any case, you will not lose anything from the trial, and you can go back at any stage, even in the middle of your first book, during that trial.

FAST READING VERSUS SLOW READING

4

📖 Fast reading helps you not only to finish reading the book quickly but also to focus on the sections of the book that you consider important. Feel free to slow your reading a little when you feel the importance of a section or even a paragraph of a book.

📖 Fast reading is an advantage but not a necessity in itself unless you are sitting for a heavy exam full of long, complex questions and of short duration. Even then, more important than fast reading is concentration and comprehension accuracy.

📖 If you are a slow reader, rather than waiting so long to reach the end of a book and start a new one, it might be better to read more than one book at the same time. This can help you to avoid getting bored.

📖 Don't be alarmed if you are a slow reader as long as you absorb what you're reading and enjoy it. But it's OK to try to learn fast reading skills to improve your reading speed and not necessarily to compete for a fast reading record.

📖 Don't hesitate to take advantage of your knack for speed-reading to reread books when you feel you haven't fully absorbed or enjoyed them from the first reading.

📖 In reading, the most important thing is accurate and thorough comprehension, not primarily speed. But if you have the gift of fast reading, you generally don't need to slow down unless you notice that you are speeding at the expense of understanding.

📖 If you are a slow reader and aspire to improve your reading speed, choose the areas of reading that are closest to your heart as you try speed-reading exercises.

📖 If you are a slow reader and cannot improve your reading speed, do not be discouraged. You can remedy that by passing through, or even skipping, the parts you feel are less important in a book that you should finish reading quickly.

📖 If you are an average reader and want to improve your skills, instead of looking for speed-reading exercises, focus on developing your concentration and comprehension skills while reading.

By focusing on the topic you're reading and preoccupying yourself in sensing the pleasure of reading, you will automatically find yourself reading at your optimum speed and not bothering to ask whether your reading is slow or fast.

FAT BOOKS VERSUS SLIM BOOKS

5

📖 Just as you should not judge a book by its cover, you cannot judge a book by its number of pages.

📖 You will miss out on a lot of pleasure and many benefits when you enter the experience of reading a slim book with the same preparation and way you read a fat book, and vice versa.

📖 Do not let the book's length mislead you. Neither the benefits gained in general nor even specifically the number of new pieces of information you could learn depend on a book's page count in any way; let alone the pleasure which cannot be measured by any such material factor.

📖 Never be ashamed to declare that you prefer slim books to fat books, as long as the former inspire you deeply and satisfy you absolutely.

📖 An excellent reader of fat books is probably not an excellent reader of slim books, and vice versa. This shouldn't be a problem for either of them as long as both enjoy what they read.

📖 Slim books are not synonymous with light-content books, and fat books are not synonymous with heavy-content books.

📖 If you are a lover of slim books, don't freak out about a fat book. You can read it as a collection of slim books, or even pick out what you like within the fat book and just deal with the selection as if you were reading one slim book.

📖 If you are a lover of fat books, do not let your preconceived ideas about slim books keep you away from reading them on the pretext that they will not satisfy your craving for reading. You can read several slim books together as if reading one fat book. You can even read one slim book as if reading a single interesting chapter of a fat book.

📖 If you find yourself taking much longer than the average estimate to read a slim book based on its page count, don't panic. If there are no external factors affecting the reading process, then pay attention. This is probably evidence that the content of the book is greater than what its volume indicates.

If you feel the urge to change the direction of your reading from fat books to slim books, or vice versa, never hesitate. Do not succumb to remorse for a type of books that you have long been familiar with. What matters in the end is your love and loyalty to reading itself, regardless of the book length.

READING A POORLY WRITTEN BOOK

6

📖 "Poorly written" is a judgment, not a categorization. You are the one making that judgment. There is no reason to be afraid of reading any book. Just try to be as objective in your judgment as possible.

📖 Even if you are a beginner, don't be afraid to read a book that may be poorly written. Your reading insight will extract the useful and discard the superfluous through an innate sieve, and you will probably not realize that automatic filtration.

📖 Even with a well-written book, you don't have to accept everything it says. You need to keep your critical senses sharp in order to agree, disagree, or comment on everything you read, no matter what level of writing and regardless of the nature of opinions and views; and with more confidence in your insights each time.

📖 Do not give in to the judgments of others, whatever those judgments are. Make sure to put your own opinion on the book after reading it. And do not hesitate to review and change your judgment whenever you feel the need to do so after rereading or during any subsequent review of the book.

📖 Referring to some books as "well-written" does not mean that the rest are poorly written, as the former is an expression of appreciation for outstanding books, while the rest can be evaluated as okay or ordinary. Do not rush to call a book poorly written just because you did not like it or because you think there are other books that are better.

📖 Don't get too worried. A book that really deserves the designation "poorly written" often exposes itself quickly.

📖 Don't be alarmed when you see that a professional evaluated a book you like as poorly written. The issue is often so relative that another professional could describe the same book as being well written. Don't let other people's opinions change your assessment of any issue, no matter who those other people are and no matter what the issue is.

📖 Regardless of the relativity of the evaluation, a person who writes a bad book is not necessarily a bad writer. Don't be in a rush to decide not to read another of that author's books.

📖 Even when you are firmly convinced that what you have read was poorly written, do not let that stop you from extracting even a single benefit from what you have read. That benefit could be nothing more than developing the skill of judging what is poor.

📖 Judging books as being poorly or well written changes, of course, from one group of people to another and from one person to another. However, the most important factor affecting judgment of writing seems to be time, especially when the judgment relates to the general mood of reading rather than being based on objective justifications. Even the objective justifications seem to relate to time.

AVID READING

7

📖 "Avid reader" is not necessarily an honorable title or, of course, an accusation. Enjoy that title if you have acquired it without being ostentatious. And do not grieve losing it if you missed it in any way.

📖 Brain cells are just like muscles. They grow with intellectual nutrition and training and wither with starvation.

📖 There is no limit to the number of pages or books you can read, as long as you are able to ingest and digest them satisfactorily.

📖 It's okay to compare yourself with others, but it's more important to have a self-comparison on which to base yourself to improve and develop your reading skills.

📖 In reading, a little continuous work is better than a lot that is discontinuous.

📖 Let your concept of avid reading be more qualitative than quantitative.

📖 When avid reading is about quantity, don't be shy about counting the number of times you've reread a book.

📖 Avid reading is not just about reading as many new books as possible. Rereading is not without benefit. It is sometimes a necessity to deepen the understanding of what you missed in the first reading.

📖 Avid reading is a talent that deserves thankfulness but one that also requires attention in terms of the variety of reading topics and the quality of the chosen books.

📖 The most critical symptom that calls for attention with regard to avid reading is losing reading pleasure and continuing just as if it were an addiction.

READING COVER TO COVER

8

📖 There is no reason for you feel forced to read cover to cover unless you are going to sit for an exam and want to get full marks.

📖 In your reading in general, do not take upon yourself the need to finish reading a book that you are bored with and your only motive for reading it is an obsession to add it to the list of books you have completed.

📖 It's important to go through the book quickly so you can better decide if you need to read it cover to cover or just read some chapters or parts of it.

📖 Reading cover to cover does not necessarily mean that you have to stick to the order it is presented. In many cases, depending on your need or mood, you can start from a chapter in the middle of the book and then go back to the first and jump to the end, and so on.

📖 The best books are not necessarily the ones that motivated you to read them from cover to cover. Rather, they are the ones that left a deep impression on you and kept inspiring you even with a single sentence.

📖 If you can't read every book in life, why do you insist on reading every book that lies in your hands cover to cover?

📖 Even when you decide to read a book cover to cover, that doesn't mean you have to finish it in one session or even in several successive sessions. Let the book take its time. Give it the attention it deserves, even if you have to intersperse your reading with a few other urgent or necessary readings.

📖 You can still cover what the book is intended for without reading it cover to cover. Learning to focus on the important parts by jumping over redundant paragraphs, or even jumping over the less important pages, is an important skill. But it needs the parallel skill of determining what should be skipped accurately and quickly.

📖 Even when you come back to a book you haven't read cover to cover, it doesn't mean you should read the parts you missed if you still think they are worth skipping. You can still then focus on what you liked and felt important for you and just reread it.

📖 The main reason not to read every book cover to cover is to save your time and energy for other readings that are more pleasant and beneficial for you.

JUDGING A BOOK BY ITS COVER

9

📖 The cover is an indispensable entry point for reading the book.

📖 The cover is made to protect the book, but its design is supposed to reflect the book's content. It is okay, then, to judge a book by its cover, but that judgment should not go beyond a kind of a fleeting impression and an aesthetic and expressive taste.

📖 It's a good idea for the book to start engaging the reader vigorously with the cover, whether through an interactive, motivational title's syntax or an inspirational, commentary-attracting design.

📖 The idea of a book cover does not have to refer directly to its content. On the contrary, sometimes indirect thoughts are more attractive. It is wise to take this into consideration before deciding to judge a book by its cover.

📖 Instead of judging a book by its cover, judge the cover itself.

📖 In addition to being an indication of the content in one way or another, it is good to look at the cover in a parallel way as if it were an independent creation, whether in terms of the connotation of the title selection or the pure artistic design.

📖 No matter how hard and smart you work to design the cover, it will not satisfy everyone whether as an entry to reading the book or even as an independent piece of art.

📖 The designer should not only read the title. It is important for him or her to read the book or at least go through it if he or she aspires to create an attractive cover with deep significance.

📖 The deliberately misleading title and cover design, to gain more readers and achieve popularity, may have adverse long-term effects regarding the credibility of the content, both for the publisher and the author. Misleading cover design may attract non-target readers who are not really interested in the book. Conversely, it may alienate the book's main target audience.

📖 It is good for the designer to be flexible to provide more than one genuinely different cover design to allow the publisher and author to choose comfortably among them. But with focus, passion, and open-mindedness about the expectations of the author and the audience, a satisfying and distinctive cover can be created efficiently without the need for many attempts.

ADDICTION TO READING A SPECIFIC GENRE

10

In general, you are fine as long as you read, no matter what genre you read and how long you spend reading only that genre.

It is useful, and even important, to diversify your areas of reading. But this is not an urgent necessity if you find yourself attracted to a genre that interests you strongly. Just be alert to any opportunity that arises to break out of your closed reading circle and seize it immediately.

Feel free to occasionally force attempts to change your reading area, or at least to freshen the air by opening windows for other parallel readings. Do not despair if you fail on the first and second attempts. Repeat the attempt from time to time and consider modifying the targeted genres and authors each time.

During your forced attempts to break your reading circle within a single preferred genre, don't worry when you find yourself struggling to finish reading a book in the new genre. You can stop reading that book at any moment and try reading another book of a different genre, or even go back to your favorite genre. The important thing is that you do not stop repeating the attempt. Remember that all genres and all books are yours to choose from whenever you like.

If after many attempts you find yourself unable to break out of the reading confinement of your preferred genre, that is no cause for major concern. Just strive hard to diversify your readings within the genre you prefer. Do not give in to the influence of certain subcategories and titles or the names of a few authors.

When you are thinking of expanding from your preferred genre, don't just consider genres that are close to it in form. You may find interest in completely different genres or even in entirely distant areas of reading.

You will never lose no matter how many times you try to go beyond reading only one genre. At the least, you'll probably come back to reading your favorite genre with more enthusiasm.

The time you pause reading, for whatever reason, is probably the best time to inspire you to find a new genre or a fresh field to read in.

📖 It is not always a question of looking for a way out of your addicted genre's reading circle. You can utilize your passion for this genre to motivate others to love it and to love reading in general.

📖 Remember that being daring to deviate from what you are familiar with in reading does not mean that you will read what you do not like. Rather, you will expand the range of books and readings you may like.

📖 Just as a destiny made you fall in love with the genre you are addicted to reading, another destiny can make you fall in love with another genre. Seek that destiny to expand your circles of knowledge and pleasure.

READING IN ANOTHER LANGUAGE

11

📖 It's never too late. If you missed learning a second language in the past, no matter how long it has been, do not despair of achieving this and benefiting from it in expanding your horizons in reading and other life aspects, whatever your level of second–language proficiency would be.

📖 Do not despair no matter how much you fail. Try again, either with the same new language you are trying to learn or with another language. Breaking into other languages is not just a linguistic skill. It is an openness to the amazing realms of knowledge, perception, and taste in all aspects of life.

📖 If you miss learning a second language or more for any reason, do not miss reading translated books on the literature and other knowledge aspects of other languages by distinguished translators. This will help you to get closer to those cultures, and even to the ways of linguistic expression in these languages, thus opening up the world in a much better way than judging it through the window of your language and culture alone.

📖 In addition to the greater number of readings available to you, and additional acquired general knowledge the other language allows, creatively enriching expression in your own language is one of the greatest trophies of reading in a language other than your mother tongue.

📖 We learn the new language letter by letter, word by word. Then we learn simple idioms and sentences mostly literally. Astonishing horizons of linguistic spoils then open before us in style and expression that can add to our mother tongues and deepen our abilities to express ourselves and the world in a richer way.

📖 If you are not fluent in reading in a second language, don't let that stop you from continuing to read in it, even if you feel annoyed by the slowness and decreased pleasure of reading because of the difficulty of the language. Continue reading mainly in your mother tongue, and dedicate some spare time—even just a little—to reading in the second language so that you develop your reading skills in it and obtain the great benefits of being open to another culture.

📖 No matter how hard the translator works to maintain the accuracy and integrity of the original text, he or she inserts his or her own understanding and perception in many areas. Reading the original text in the author's mother tongue makes you the master of the situation to create your own concept of the text away from any guardianship or medium.

📖 The translator does not always deliberately betray the original text, and the issue is not necessarily that he or she reflects his or her own perception of the text spontaneously. The biggest challenge is the language itself. Any language carries more than one meaning for one word and carries for one meaning many words and expressions. Reading the text in its original language provides the perfect opportunity to deal with such language challenges.

📖 Translation mislays much of the linguistic value of some texts that depend mainly on style, rhythm of words and sentences, and wordplay, such as lyrical poetry. Therefore, it becomes unavoidable to read such works in the authors' mother tongues to realize their literary value.

📖 Being proficient in reading in a second language increases reading opportunities for you. The benefits also increase by making it possible to access translations from all other languages through the second language you master.

WHEN WILL YOU BENEFIT FROM READING A BOOK?

12

📖 You begin to benefit from the book while reading it when you feel the pleasure of reading, and perhaps even before that when you can't wait to get a copy of it after hearing an encouraging comment about it. Deep pleasure is the highest value a book can give you even before start reading it.

📖 It is unlikely you will never get any benefits from reading a book. But assuming that it might have happened once, there's no reason you shouldn't get anything beneficial out of reading another book.

📖 You will feel the benefits of reading a book equal to how much you liked that book. So be sure to pick what you like. In the worst case, look for what might be attractive and enjoyable in the subject you find yourself reading anyway.

📖 You often read a book expecting to achieve a specific goal, but then benefit in one or more areas that are completely unexpected.

📖 You'll get the most value out of a book when you don't keep your expectations too narrow. Allow the book to inspire you without prior restrictions.

📖 Sometimes you go back to a book you read a long time ago and then wonder: *Did I really read this book?* Don't be alarmed. It's normal, and our memories often don't keep everything ready to be retrieved. But the benefits of reading and all life's deeper experiences remain in the subconscious in one form or another and amenable to inspiration.

📖 Benefiting from reading any book is not like the return on an investment that you expect during a specific period, making you a loser if it were delayed beyond that period. The returns on investment in reading books are extended and renewed throughout life.

📖 To disagree strongly with what you have read is one of the most prominent signs that you have benefited from the book, providing that such disagreement motivates you to think more deeply regarding the discussed ideas.

📖 Don't be alarmed when you find that what you came out with after reading a book is different from what others who read the same book discovered. On the contrary, this is something of which to be proud. It is evidence that you read the book your own way.

DO READING HABITS CHANGE OVER TIME? 13

📖 The most important thing, before worrying about the habits that accompany reading, is that reading itself should become a well-established habit for you.

📖 It is natural and useful that your reading habits change over time. Everything around you changes. Changing your habits on any level is, to some degree, important so that they fit smoothly into the changing aspects of your life.

📖 If you find that your reading habits have been remarkably stable for an extended period, there is nothing to be alarmed about. Don't take coercive steps to change your reading habits as long as they don't overwhelm your life or delay your smooth progress in any respect. There is no need to change what is going well just for the sake of change. But do not hesitate to make changes if you are filled with a desire for renewal and have the vision and ability to create a refreshing and stimulating renewal.

📖 When you feel monotonous or need to change your reading habits for any reason, it is a good idea to start with a small adjustment and work your way up to the change you want. For example, if reading at night is affecting your sleep quality, you can adjust your nightly reading time to one hour earlier and so on until you have enough to finish your reading session before preparing for a quiet and deep sleep.

📖 If a gradual change in reading habits doesn't work, sometimes the opposite is required. Make a dramatic change. For example, eliminate the evening reading period entirely and replace it with reading at the beginning of the day or during intermittent periods throughout the day.

📖 Changes in reading habits are often not limited to reading scheduled times but also extended to include reading duration. Perhaps the changes are more obvious regarding favorite reading topics.

📖 Don't be alarmed if your average reading rate decreases with age. It is natural that the peak of avid reading is during the early stages of youth. Then the readings become more selective as needed and often more qualitative.

📖 It is okay to have habits that encourage reading and make it a more enjoyable experience. But watch these habits carefully. Some may become rituals that bind you and make it difficult to read without performing them.

📖 Do not worry about the effects of reading habits outside your control, such as emergency health conditions. Be prepared to accept the psychological impact of compelling circumstances and be prepared to deal with them calmly by adopting the best practical solutions you can. For example, when visual impairment is clearly hindering you, try to get used to audiobooks, no matter how hard it may have seemed to you before.

📖 When you find yourself far away from reading, it is okay to create reading habits that encourage you to return to reading. Take care that these habits do not have an undesirable effect in the long run. In general, try to make your habits sustainable.

STOP READING FOR A WHILE

14

📖 Don't worry if you feel inclined to stopping reading for any length of time. To stop reading does not mean to stop thinking.

📖 Look at any period of stopping reading, whether compulsive or intentional, as if it were a recovery period in which you regain your mental fitness after a long status of reading glut.

📖 A reading pause is useful and refreshing, especially when it is not for a long time. But that does not mean it is mandatory if you find yourself reading with interest and pleasure and do not feel any annoying restrictions on the rest of your life aspects.

📖 A reading pause provides time to reflect on what you have read and what you can do next. Feel free to ask yourself during the reading pause any relevant question you encounter, even if the question is about the usefulness of reading in general. Don't worry; this is the best period to ask questions about reading in general and to get convincing answers.

📖 If you take a long break from reading without accomplishing anything, including positively reviewing your previous reading performance and refreshing your mind, it is best to push yourself back to reading, not necessarily all at once but at least gradually.

📖 Don't let the illusion of giving up reading and pursuing any other hobby or work occupy you during reading pause period. Reading is not a full-time job or a job you perform along with other work. Rather, it is a healthy mental practice that permeates your life in all its aspects in the way you see fit.

📖 Use your reading pause to discover new authors from different perspectives and horizons. Add some of their books to your want-to-read list for when you come back to reading.

📖 Thinking or dreaming about writing must have knocked on the minds of every reader in one way or another. Don't worry if you find yourself unable to write professionally. Deep reading actually involves rewriting the read text in view of the reader's critical questions and interactive relationship with the text. Just be sure to express your questions and interactions in a simple way to get involved in rewriting the text, or even coming up with innovative ideas. Reading pause is a good chance to evaluate such potential and enhance the possibility for relevant achievement.

📖 If during a specifically timed reading pause you feel an urgent desire to return to reading a book before that period expires, do not hesitate to do so. You can count that return to reading a particular book as if it were a time out from the reading break itself. Resume the rest of the break later, after you finish reading the book. Otherwise, you can be satisfied with that amount of reading pause if you feel that it has achieved its goals early and you have taken the necessary recovery to return with a new spirit to continue reading.

📖 A reading break should not only end with returning to reading refreshed with a new spirit and a scattered set of lessons learned. It is also best to have at the end of the break an overall updated reading regime interspersed with reading breaks as felt useful and further needed.

15

A UNIQUE CONTEST

📖 If reading must be a contest, it is certainly not about who reads a greater number of pages or books.

📖 It is okay to participate in reading contests, strive to win first place, and enjoy the trance of victory. But the most important thing is to continue exploring and achieving some of the genuine knowledge purposes away from showy reading and the thrill of breaking records.

📖 There is an inescapable amount of ostentation that exists within all of us. But don't let bragging grow and overwhelm you so that it appears as if it were a fundamental motivator for your actions.

📖 Reading, in particular, loses a lot of its value as a result of ostentation, whether on the intellectual level or on a purely personal one.

📖 Reading contests are not purposes in themselves. If you find yourself pushed for any reason to participate in a contest, do not miss using that as an opportunity to strengthen your skills in some aspect of reading.

📖 Strive to get inspired in reading contests by those who demonstrate outstanding qualitative abilities in the challenge, not necessarily by the one who was ranked the first place.

📖 You don't necessarily need to wait for any reading contests, which all have their terms and conditions that are indispensable for any competition. Create the reading challenge you desire and race yourself in the areas and skills of reading you need in your own way.

📖 If you find yourself wanting, or even compelled, to take on a reading contest, don't just focus on what will get you to first place. Focus on what makes you stand out in your own way.

📖 It is easy to decide who has read more, but it is hard to judge who has read better.

📖 In reading contests it is important to focus on what the judges want. But amid the challenge, do not forget it is your love of books and your devotion to reading that will essentially save you in critical competition situations. Most important, your love of books and your devotion to reading are what will remain as assets and constant motivations when the competition ends, whatever the outcome.

HOW DO YOU REVIEW A BOOK?

16

📖 Your review of any book should reflect your opinion about whether the book achieved its purpose, not about whether you liked the book or not.

📖 No review can cover everything that can be said about the book. The important thing is to present the idea of the book in general and then show the most important of what you see as done well and what could have been better.

📖 Getting rid of prejudices helps you to write an objective review that benefits the reader and does not detract from the book's value.

📖 Not only negative prejudices, but also the excessive bias toward the book may not make the review convincing to the reader and cause the opposite results than what you want. Calmness and prudence are essential in all cases.

📖 If for whatever reason you cannot get rid of your prejudices concerning the book, at least try to present objectively what makes you insist on those judgments.

📖 Using a number of stars to rate the book is not necessary. But if you must, make sure that your rating reflects as accurately as possible what you detailed in the review so as not to confuse the reader.

📖 Previous opinions and reviews affect you in some way and their influence cannot be completely eliminated. Do not worry about that. Rather, try to benefit from it as material that enriches your review with more comments.

📖 It is important that you read the book carefully to provide a valuable review. But if you felt eager to comment on a book after quickly scrolling through it, do not forget to highlight that in your comment. And most important, mention what prompted you to scroll quickly through the book and what drew your attention to the general or detailed notes on some points in the book.

📖 It is not the main purpose of reviews to direct people to read the book or not to read it. But it is okay to suggest the type of people who would most likely enjoy and benefit from reading the book.

No matter how busy or hurried you are, don't miss an opportunity to write a comment on what you have read, even if it is just one line or two carefully chosen words. This is the right of the book and its readers of you, and it is your duty toward yourself as a serious reader.

ISN'T THE E-BOOK A REAL BOOK?

17

📖 The e-book has become an impressive reality, regardless of whether it will replace the paper book or not.

📖 Some readers not only insist on the e-book and reject the paper book, they request a specific electronic format rather just any type of e-book.

📖 The bias shown by some toward the electronic book, and the reluctance and nostalgia that others feel about paper books, is likely similar to what was going on when the paper book replaced the reading media that preceded it.

📖 Disagreement and controversy over the acceptance or rejection of the e-book probably appeared similarly every time there was a change in the form of the paper book itself, whether in terms of size, paper material, or even printing in color versus black only.

📖 The e-book is definitely not the end. An entirely or somewhat different new reading medium will appear, so the debate will be renewed, and people will be seized by conflicting states of enthusiasm for the new and nostalgia for the old.

📖 The paper book seems to be a stubborn fighter. Despite the power of the electronic book and the ease of its spread and circulation, the paper book remains strongly present, whether as the medium many reading lovers still prefer, or as an additional—and perhaps essential—copy alongside the electronic version of the same book.

📖 A paper book retains many advantages that an e-book does not provide despite its own advantages. However, the existence of the paper book seems to be linked to nostalgia and getting used to a particular form of reading more than to the irreplaceable advantages of the paper book.

📖 Regardless of the extent of the survival of the paper book and the strength of its presence, the coming days seem as if they are moving strongly in favor of the electronic book, given the integration of the idea of dealing through what is electronic in all fields. For example, it is much easier to copy from e-books for the purpose of citation or sharing of commentary, which also applies to e-writing. This in particular strengthens the position of the e-book.

The e-book has not only become a reality but a reality that has gone beyond imagination, both in terms of the incredible speed of spread and circulation, and the massive storage spaces that have been astoundingly and incomparably decreased.

In any case, and apart from what nostalgia imposes or even the persisting practical advantages, the paper book will remain as much as what will remain from a tangible reality in our lives versus a virtual reality.

18

READING VERSUS OTHER MEANS OF KNOWLEDGE

📖 The book is certainly not the only means of knowledge, but it seems to be the most famous of knowledge means when it comes to the direct reception of knowledge.

📖 The deepest means of knowledge are undoubtedly life experiences, which surpass books in value because they only make knowledge possible through harsh practical trials. In addition, life experiences are forced on everyone, each according to their personalities and lifestyles, while books offer optional knowledge according to the person's inclinations and desire to read.

📖 Books are still distinguished by the direct, fast information and knowledge they provide to the reader, which clearly exceeds what any person can acquire from knowledge of life experiences, no matter how he or she lived and had different experiences.

📖 Traveling is one of the most amazing and enriching means of knowledge. The deepest benefits of travel are not your immediate observations and notes but rather what settles in your subconscious and inspires you throughout the long run, perhaps without you directly realizing it.

📖 In the not-too-distant past, radio, television, and cinema offered unique and amazing prospects for knowledge. Today the internet contains all these means, including the book itself, incomparably in terms of the volume and speed of the information and knowledge flow.

📖 The book still has good reasons for its continuing sway and charm against the e-book, and even in comparison to the internet in general. You can still, for example, hold the book and enjoy all its benefits no matter how long the power supply is cut off.

📖 The book is still so cunning that it spreads the illusion it is the means of knowledge best able to provide the most useful and simple information. This is evident when the markets are flooded with books that introduce the reader to the internet and its history, claiming to simplify its complexities.

📖 The most valuable means of knowledge are those who have experience and wisdom around you, especially the elderly. Take advantage of their presence by giving them the deserved attention and appreciation.

📖 Your experiences are some of the richest and most reliable sources of knowledge. Do not stop reviewing and evaluating these experiences deliberately in order to draw lessons from them and progress more steadily and confidently in the future.

📖 The deepest means of knowledge are an open mind and soul.

Printed in the United States
by Baker & Taylor Publisher Services